In this book, Rita-Marie is looking at her journey and her experiences, which has become her story. In it she has included helpful information and insights which hopefully helps you on your journey when the time comes.

I have watched her develop and grow throughout the years we have known each other. May she continue to grow and bloom in her future.

Nerida Thompson
Former Funeral Director
July 1984 to December 2016

I have known Rita-Marie since childhood; she has always been very thoughtful and empathic towards others. I am extremely proud of Rita-Marie, and her lifetime of supporting family, friends, and the wider community in their darkest hours.

I only wish I had read Creating a Fond Farewell *prior to my Mother-in-law's death in January 2021. Under the influence of difficult family members, and not wanting to upset others, my husband and I 'put-up' with the arrangements made. It sure will be different when we go!*

Congratulations to Rita-Marie, on writing a long-overdue and informative book to help people negotiate the worst time of their life. I enjoyed reading this book immensely and read it again and again. It is written in a simple, explanatory style, and I'm planning on putting a copy aside with my requests to help my children when the time comes. Hopefully they won't have to suffer the same heartache I did.

Raelee Painter (née Black)
formally of Winton, Queensland

In her introduction to the book Rita-Marie says she wants to share the art of saying goodbye. She has done exactly this. I love the way Rita-Marie has shared her journey and lessons through her stories. They are beautiful stories that will make you laugh, leave you thinking, move you to tears and, most importantly, inform. Death, grief, funerals, are all words that many people have a hard time coping with. Read this book—share it with your family and friends. By the end of the book, you will find that those words are not so scary, you will be informed, comforted and have clarity to make decisions when the fond farewell comes.

Trish Springsteen
Get Known Be Seen Specialist

CREATING

A

FOND FAREWELL

RITA-MARIE LENTON

Creating a Fond Farewell
Copyright © 2022 Rita-Marie Lenton
First published 2022

Rita-Marie Lenton
SoulCrystalEarth
32 Trafalgar Drive
Kippa-Ring QLD 4021
www.soulcrystalearth.com.au

Self-published with technical guidance and support from Deborah Fay and the Authorpreneurs Bootcamp at Disruptive Publishing.

Editing Services by Jandyco
Book Cover by Rita-Marie Lenton in Canva
Layout by Jo Scott
Author's Headshot courtesy Joseph Fay Film & Photo Co.

All rights reserved. Without limiting the rights under Copyright reserved above, no part of this publication may be reproduced, stored in, or introduced into a database and retrieval system, or transmitted in any form or by any means (electronic, mechanical, photocopying, recording or otherwise) without the prior written permission of both the owner of the Copyright and the above publishers.

ISBN# 978-0-6456110-0-7 Print
ISBN# 978-0-6456110-1-4 eBook

Author's Note

This book is a first-person account of my many years of practice as a funeral director. The stories are from my own personal experiences within the funeral industry and in no way reflect upon how any specific funeral company operates. They are my particular recollections of the events contained in this book.

My intention in writing this book is to share with you the art of saying a meaningful goodbye to a loved one—*of creating a fond farewell.*

I have written in the spirit of openness, so that you will come to understand the many options, and the range of possibilities, available to you when the time comes to arrange a funeral.

This book is in no way a criticism of the funeral industry; on the contrary, it is a guide to help the average person navigate their way through, what can be, a confronting and challenging time. At its heart, the funeral industry is a caring and compassionate profession providing an essential service to people in their darkest hours. Knowing how to engage with the process to create a sincere and meaningful farewell, benefits everyone.

I have chosen to omit some of the names of people and organisations that I refer to in the book. This has been done, with due care and consideration, to protect the privacy of those individuals or entities. Where I have used names, it is with the express permission of those persons or organisations concerned.

I am not a financial advisor—any suggestions or information regarding funeral insurances and funeral bonds (Chapter 14) are my personal view on the products. The information contained in this book is general in nature and does not take into account your personal situation. You should consider whether the information is appropriate to your needs, and where appropriate, seek professional advice from a financial adviser before entering into any contract regarding these products.

In the final pages I have listed a resource library to assist you to locate relevant organisations. They encompass the process from planning and conducting a funeral to providing grief counselling. Readers are advised to check for similar organisations in their state of Australia, as there may be different requirements and regulations between states. While these references are Australia-specific, readers in other countries can be assured that similar organisations exist worldwide, and they can generally be located via a quick internet search.

Rita-Marie Lenton

CREATING A FOND FAREWELL

RITA-MARIE LENTON

Understanding the choices and options we have ... when someone dies

I dedicate this book to my mother,

Florence Alma Maud Porter, formerly Kelly, née Ewan.

Without her in my life I would not have understood the intuitive side to my nature. Mum always had an uncanny way about her when someone was going to cross over.

Without my mother's passing, I would not have managed the many moments of understanding while dealing with a family in crisis.

Table of Contents

Foreword 1

Introduction 3

CHAPTER ONE 11

Learning on the job to be a receptionist 11

CHAPTER TWO 13

Becoming the Funeral Director 13

CHAPTER THREE 23

Becoming the Manager 23

CHAPTER FOUR 25

Creating the Fond Farewell 25

CHAPTER FIVE 31

Children Attending Funerals 31

CHAPTER SIX 39

Some of my most memorable funerals 39

CHAPTER SEVEN 55

Being an intuitive and empathic individual 55

CHAPTER EIGHT 59

Being the funeral director and the celebrant 59

CHAPTER NINE 63

Funerals in the time of COVID-19 63

CHAPTER TEN 69

Organising the Funeral Service. 69

CHAPTER ELEVEN 73

Funerals: Attended or Non-attended 73

CHAPTER TWELVE 77

Burial or Cremation 77

CHAPTER THIRTEEN 87

Choosing the Celebrant, Priest, or Pastor 87

CHAPTER FOURTEEN 89

Prearranging Your Funeral. 89

CHAPTER FIFTEEN 95

Don't let your story die with you 95

Resource Library 99

About the Author 101

Acknowledgements 103

More by the same Author 105

What's Next from Rita-Marie? 107

Foreword

I was introduced to Rita-Marie Lenton when I entered into Funeral Service in April 2007.

At that time Rita-Marie had been in the industry for seven years.

My journey from Funeral Assistant to Funeral Arranger and Conductor saw the next seven years working in the same company as Rita-Marie and I witnessed the changing roles in her career.

In my 15 years of service, Rita-Marie has supported me as a mentor, colleague, confidante, and most importantly, a friend.

Today, I serve as the Customer Services Manager of a funeral home alongside a team of 34 dedicated Funeral Care workers.

Funeral Care is an industry like no other. Each Funeral Care worker has their own collection of very personal and unique memories.

In the pages before you, Rita-Marie shares her own story in her own words: how she was called into Funeral Care, to the changing roles throughout her career. Rita-Marie shares stories that provoke thought and serve to teach. The privilege of service, the emotions she faced, and the sometimes-unexplainable experiences encountered when caring for families.

Creating a Fond Farewell

Testament to this are the families who, with grace, have allowed their loved one's stories to be shared in these pages and Rita-Marie's role in creating a fond farewell for them.

May their loved ones be remembered always.

Yours in service

Carla Hitchcock
Customer Services Manager
— Funeral Industry

Introduction

I believe Linda Ellis summed up life in her poem *The Dash*. When I reflect upon her words, she asks a valid question of us to consider our lives and the lives of our loved ones.

At the end of your days what will you be remembered for the most? Was it your house, your cars, or your cash?

I would like to believe it was the way you made people feel!

In this day and age, we have lost the art of saying farewell and the understanding of why we have the need to say goodbye in a meaningful, creative, and memorable manner.

Let me introduce myself. My name is Rita-Marie Lenton, I am going to share with you the art of saying goodbye. My main purpose is to show you the many options available when you lose someone.

I will share with you my stories, what I have learnt along the way, and what you need to know to have a meaningful goodbye. Most people do not know the range of possibilities available to them when the time comes to arrange a funeral.

I am writing this book because I don't want anyone to go through what happened when my mother passed away. We were all so unprepared for the emotions of intense grief and anger. We certainly didn't understand too much about the practical side of arranging her funeral. Even worse, we didn't know what we needed to know when that time came.

I have worked in the funeral industry for over 21 years as a funeral director, a manager, and a crematorium manager. The next stage in my career, as a funeral celebrant, has already begun.

I am taking you with me on my journey, and I will show you how I fell into this rewarding, challenging, and satisfying career.

To explain my story, I have to go back to the beginning. Death was a natural part of life for me. What I did not understand was the *why*.

Why, could I not attend the funeral of my great Aunt Alice? It was just not done in those days. I loved her, I missed her, where did she go? Why could I not be there? All these questions rambled around in my young mind, with no answers.

When my friend died in a car accident, I was only seven years old, and I could hear the adults talking. When I heard the mother of the boy telling my mum how she held him in her arms, and he would not wake up, I did not understand. Where was he now? Why couldn't I see him? It was the same old story: *children should be seen and not heard*.

Moving forward a couple of more years and my great-grandmother, passed away. Once again, my parents would not let me go to the funeral—again it was the old adage of *children should be seen and not heard*.

Introduction

When my cousin took his own life, and me being such a young child of nine-going-on-ten, I was once again not allowed to attend the funeral.

However, those times, of being denied the chance to attend funerals and understand the processes of why we need to say goodbye, never stopped me from hanging out at our local cemetery. You would often find me sitting at the grave of my great-grandmother. When life got tough, Granma was my go-to person, she was the one I turned to when I wanted to tell someone all my troubles.

My acceptance, and being comfortable, with the topic of death showed itself in other ways. When I was in grade five, aged around the age of ten, the teacher posed a question relating to finding the dead centre of town. School was not my strong point, so I wasn't always the first to answer. All the students in the class got very technical measuring out the area of the town, some students went as far as measuring out the shire. When the teacher asked me for my answer, well, the class just laughed; they knew I was not the brightest star in the class, yet the teacher politely told them I was correct! Yes, you guessed it, I had written down that the cemetery is the *dead centre* of any town or community.

When I was in grade seven, the nuns requested the grade seven children to sing in the choir at the funeral of a prominent person in the community. I was touched by the whole process of the mass and listening to the story of her life, I found it to be a very moving experience. When it came time for the coffin to be carried from the church, we all formed a guard of honour before having to return to the classroom. This was the first funeral service I had ever attended, despite having been exposed to death many times in my young life. I just did not understand why younger children were never allowed to be involved. I found the whole experience both moving and respectful. Who knew this would become my profession?

In 1996, when my mother's illness had taken a turn for the worse, none of us knew what to do or how to go about organising a funeral—let alone who to talk to. It was my eldest Great Aunt, upon finding out that my mother was in hospital in Rockhampton, who insisted I was to contact mum's cousin who was then the owner of Fitzroy Funerals. Our mum, *God bless her cotton socks*, would never discuss her choices. The only comment she ever made was *"just chuck me under a log in the backyard".* Not very legal or practical, especially in this day and age—and absolutely no help in guiding us as to what her preferences were.

This was to be the first hurdle we had to overcome; my stepfather and I wanted a cremation, while my younger sister and her family wanted a burial. Our cousin worked through our concerns and, after about half an hour, we all agreed Mum would be laid to rest by burial in the Rockhampton Memorial Garden of Remembrance. This discussion was guided by our cousin with the professional expertise, which was rare enough to make it stand out as 30 minutes well spent.

Introduction

What I was not prepared for were the emotions at the time and the anger and fighting amongst ourselves over silly little issues. I could not believe we acted the way we did, but it was because of all the angst we were feeling. This experience was to become my biggest tool when dealing with grieving families, especially the ones that were fighting amongst themselves.

As mum had died on the 22nd of December the rush to get the funeral over and done with before Christmas was the biggest regret of my life. There were so many decisions we made on the fly that could have been so different with better outcomes for us all.

I can never dig my mother up again and recreate the service.

I fell into the biggest trap of not allowing my youngest daughter to attend the funeral. She had just started her first job and it would have been difficult for her to get time off work.

I also wanted to protect my daughter from the immense fighting amongst us at the time. This is something I really regret, as she still struggles with not attending her grandmother's funeral service many years on.

I was not prepared for the graveside service or the choice of clergy. My brother did not get to be with mum when she passed, so an open coffin was arranged at the graveside—not ideal!

I was once told if you see a dead body in the coffin, to stop the memory from haunting you, just place a kiss on the forehead—bad advice! No-one prepared me for the chemical burn to my lips from the use of formaldehyde in preserving my loved one's body for this event.

The person who was to give the eulogy did not make it to the funeral, so I stepped forward and gave some sort of speech about mum's good points. To this day I still do not know what was said, but afterwards everyone congratulated me and said how well I spoke. My mind was blank.

These experiences before, during, and after my mother's funeral have shaped the personal, professional, and emotional aspects of my life in becoming a funeral director.

Let's skip forward to the year 2000. At the beginning of that year, I had begun a journey to find a job that would pay me a wage. Knowing I needed computer skills, and not having worked in an office environment for a number of years, I started the year by entering into a course at The Redcliffe TAFE, called *Re-Entry to the Workplace*.

When I was nearing the end of the course, I started looking for work. This led me to an interview at a local funeral home in Redcliffe, Queensland.

They called me two days later and told me, "While you did not get the job with us, I have passed your resumé onto the crematorium manager". I was not sure what the manager meant by that; was it for a job potentially, or did they mean to burn my resumé?

Introduction

Not long after this, I received a call from the manager of the crematorium to go for an interview. It was the beginning of April, and I was still two weeks away from finishing my course, so I sat in the interview expecting all the usual questions on my work experiences. I need not have worried, the manager said, "You have the job, just want to know when you can start". We settled on the 17th of April as I would have, by then, completed my course.

As I arrived at work on that first day, I stood on the small bridge that led to the front office and looked out over the rose garden. I felt, in that moment, I had arrived home. So began my journey into what was to be an amazing, challenging, and inspirational time of my working life.

Not all funeral directors are born into the industry and becoming a funeral director draws on so many different elements: hands-on training, experience, learning as you go. The knowledge you gain is from the experiences you have, through the families you meet, and the colleagues you work with.

CHAPTER ONE

Learning on the job to be a receptionist

When I first started working at the crematorium, my role was that of casual receptionist and memorial consultant. I was being trained by the full-time receptionist/memorial consultant to take on her work in six weeks time, as she was going on holidays.

My duties were to answer the telephones, take bookings for cremations from the funeral directors, do the paperwork for each cremation of the day, book appointments for families wanting to collect their loved one's ashes or to memorialise their loved one's ashes in our grounds, plus general office duties.

The first thing I had to get around was saying the name of the business followed by my full name. I soon learnt to shorten it after someone snored on the other end of the phone, during my long introduction to the call.

Saying *'Good Morning'* or *'Good Afternoon'* with a smile in your voice is not the way to answer the phone when someone rings about their loved one. I learnt that on the third day, when a lady gave me a dressing down for being way too cheery on the phone. She had phoned to make an appointment to collect her husband's ashes and being cheery was not the way to welcome her into that conversation.

By the fifth day I really learnt to check with the cremator operator if the ashes were ready before I told a family they could come in and pick them up straight away. This little mistake resulted in me having to process the ashes myself, in my usual approach of *'okay I can do this'*. I innocently asked, "What do, I do?" With that the operator told me to get the remains and start processing them. No instructions, so I had to guess—however I worked it out.

As a result of this startling experience, I started writing notes, so I had something to fall back on. These notes were to become *procedures* in later years for other staff members who were new to the job.

Into the third week now, and I was getting the hang of things until a lady rang to say she had a complaint. I had been told not to put people on hold on the telephone. This was because our system had no *on-hold* music, and the head consultant was worried the caller would think we had forgotten them. I put the telephone down and went to the filing cabinet to retrieve the file and, you guessed it, the lady on the telephone heard me saying "Oh shit!".

I was grateful I worked for an understanding boss who soon realised there was a gap in my training. As a result of that experience, the boss found a way to add on-hold music to the telephone system, and the policy became *'always place the caller on hold while you retrieve the file.'* Rita-Marie's Principal #1. After six weeks this was it, I was on my own—the crematorium survived, and so did I!

CHAPTER TWO

Becoming the Funeral Director

After the full-time receptionist/memorial consultant returned, I was not sure how my role within the company would develop. The company decided to make me an offer of a permanent part-time role, with 20 hours of work per week guaranteed. Over the next three years I would exceed those hours regularly as I trained between the company's different crematoriums. I found myself working more on an administrative level, including debt collections for outstanding memorial payments. It was about two years in when the company made a decision to add a funeral branch based out of the crematorium.

Enter a new manager, who was constantly looking over my shoulder and making me feel uncomfortable. He decided that I had the makings of a good funeral director, and so began the next part of my journey. To say I was not prepared would be an understatement! The first time I went to a funeral arrangement was with the new manager. We had been asked to go to the house to sit with the deceased's wife to guide her through the arrangements. I was told to complete the paperwork and just listen; the process seemed straightforward.

The next arrangement was in our office. The same basic advice was to complete the paperwork and just listen. It was after that minimal training that the manager felt I was ready to go it alone. This was the point when I sat with a family to arrange my first *direct cremation*. There is little thinking required when arranging a service like this; it is simply a case of completing the paperwork. A direct cremation is when the family do not want to have a service, they just want the funeral director to organise the cremation to take place, and they collect the ashes of their loved one at a later date.

Then came the twin babies. Luckily for me, Nerida Thompson, the manager at the Redcliffe branch, was in the office and thought it was best for her to sit in. Turns out this was to be my first really big lesson in funeral arranging. We did not meet with the parents at the time, instead, we met with the two grandmothers. Mum was still in hospital recovering and Dad was working, so they decided they would get things started. They wanted the service to be in three weeks' time to give the mother time to recuperate at home. They wanted a viewing for the parents, and the uncle was to film the entire service. The grandmothers were going to officiate at the service and another relative had put together a slide show.

When the babies arrived into our care at the main mortuary, the manager phoned me and said, *"Do you realise these babies are not in good condition?"* When I replied with some horror, *"No!"* it was because I hadn't been made aware of it by the grandmothers. He said he would do what he could, but he could not guarantee that

TWO | Becoming the Funeral Director

the babies would be viewable, as the funeral was three weeks away.

He was completely correct. On the day of the service when the babies arrived, I took the lid off the coffin and almost fainted. I quickly put the lid back on and wondered just how I was going to have a viewing, with a TV cameraman in the room; and how was I going to tell the parents, whom I was yet to meet, that their babies were not viewable?

Enter the uncle. As luck would have it, I knew him. He had filmed me a few weeks beforehand for a promotional video for the Redcliffe TAFE. I explained to him the situation, as he wanted to set up in the viewing room. He asked to see the babies. Because he was the Dad's uncle, he felt he had a better chance of breaking the news to the parents. We both spoke with the Dad and then bought Mum into the room. Naturally, she was really upset and said, "If I had known this, I would have held the service sooner".

The lesson I learnt that day: no matter how caring and protective the grandmothers are, it is never good to plan for a baby's service without the parents being present to have their input.

The next funeral I arranged was for a young man who had taken his own life. The thing that affected me deeply was his dog. The family spoke about how his dog was found at the scene and he had not left his master. They explained the dog was grieving, they wanted permission to have his dog come to the funeral, and naturally the answer was, "Yes, of course you can". When they arrived for the viewing, they asked if they could bring the dog into the room. I still feel chills as I recall standing outside the door of the viewing room and hearing the cries of that dog. His grief at the loss of his master was just as real as the family's. This was my first funeral relating to suicide outside of my own family, and one of my hardest. During the service, the dog sat with coffin and the family had to pick him up and carry him from the chapel when the time came for them to leave.

As I was still just feeling my way with funeral arrangements, and still learning about the legalities around the paperwork, once again I made a mistake. The young man concerned was the son from his mother's former relationship. His legal last name was not his stepfather's last name, and I had completed the paperwork based on what the family said they wanted him to be known as. This, I soon learned, was a really big legal *no-no*! It took some time to sort out the confusion about his legal name.

This experience led to one of the funeral directors, who had attended the service at the crematorium, standing over me and shouting about how hard I had made his job when he collected the deceased from the coroner's office. While the mistake had been sorted with the family and the paperwork amended prior to the funeral, I still felt humiliated: being new to the funeral directors' position and to have a colleague unreasonably rant at me in front of other staff who weren't supportive. That was a mistake I never made again.

TWO | Becoming the Funeral Director

The lesson I learnt from that experience was to always explain to the family that we needed the *correct legal name* for the documentation. From a blended family myself, I understood the sensitivity around not wanting to use the legal names for emotional reasons. As soon as I explained that the paperwork was a legal document, families were understanding. I would always reassure them they could refer to the loved one with a different name during the service, just not on the official documentation.

Based on that experience, the company soon realised I was lacking in my training.

The company had many sites divided between the northside hub and the southside hub, on either side of the Brisbane River. Because my experience with the northside crew was not as positive as I would have liked, I was asked if I would prefer to attend training on the southside for three weeks. This helped me immensely in gaining greater knowledge of the funeral fundamentals.

It was at the beginning of my third year with the company that they realised I was only a permanent part-timer who had been working full-time hours.

I was offered to be put on full-time and transferred into the main branch on the northside of Brisbane. So began the next part of my journey; I learnt everything about funerals: from the reception area to the mortuary, to transferring the deceased from the hospitals, nursing homes, residences, and the coroner's centre. I was placed on the after-hours phone roster, which meant I was taking first-calls when someone had passed, as well as coordinating funeral arrangements and transfers over the weekends.

Covering the after-hours telephone roster at home did raise some other awkward moments. You take phone calls at all hours of the day and night; it is a challenge all funeral directors face.

One instance that comes to mind, that I would like to share with you, involves my eldest granddaughter.

I was minding my granddaughter one weekend while I had the telephones, when I had taken a call from a lady regarding her grandmother's passing. Unbeknown to me I hadn't realised that little 'Miss Three' sat on the floor next to me while I went through everything with the young lady on the other end of the phone. After the phone call had ended, our little Miss looked at me and said, "Granma, what happened to that lady's grandma?" Not wanting to sugar-coat things, I gently explained to her that the grandmother had died and was now with the angels in heaven.

The next week my daughter was asked to have a meeting with the principal of the kindy Miss Three attended. Imagine my daughter's horror when the principal said Miss Three had an unusual preoccupation with death. When my daughter asked, "What has she done?", the principal replied, "Miss Three has been telling all her classmates that their grandmothers were going to die and go to heaven".

My daughter, trying not to laugh, apologised to the principal and then went on to explain that she had been

TWO | Becoming the Funeral Director

called into work unexpectedly over the weekend. Consequently, she needed me (her mother), who is a funeral director and was looking after the funeral homes after hours phones, to look after Miss Three. We still, today, tell the story in the family about being mindful of little ones with big ears.

I was really lucky to work with some amazing colleagues who had been in the industry for a very long time. I also earned the respect of my peers. The one person I would like to pay tribute to is the mortician who trained me in the mortuary.

Bill Wiggins had grown up around the funeral industry and was the most amazing person I knew. While he was an exceptional funeral director, he was never comfortable with arranging services with the families. Bill was always great as the assistant on a service, but where he truly rocked was in the mortuary; this was his domain.

I first realised just how great he was when he took care of my mother-in-law. I had been at her bedside when she was dying, and she didn't look very nice at all. I spoke to the team and explained I really needed a viewing prior to service. Bill did such a wonderful job, my mother-in-law just looked so relaxed in the coffin. When I saw her, I could not help but compare how much better she looked compared to my mother at her own funeral—the difference was astounding.

Bill taught me to respect the deceased as if it was my own family member. He would always ask the arrangers, if possible, for a photo of the deceased so he could get the person looking just right. I still remember my first day in the mortuary when Bill introduced me to the deceased by their name. He explained to me how he talked to them and explained to them what he was doing. He also had a little habit of looking at the music the family may have chosen for the service and would try to play their favourite song.

It was always an honour to care for families, especially those of my friends'.

I remember being with Bill on a day when my friend's mother came into our care, and I requested to be the person who helped him dress her. When I arrived at the mortuary Bill said, "I will let you do her makeup". Now that was a disaster! Bill just happened to look at me and said, "What are you doing? That looks terrible!" I replied, "Bill, look at me, do you see makeup on my face?" He replied, "I had not thought about it, I just thought since you are a woman you would know how to put makeup on". After laughing about this, Bill decided he would do the makeup and I would dress her.

Over the years, I have had experiences with bringing people into care from different nursing homes, hospitals, and the coroner's office. I soon learnt with a coroner's case that smell takes on a whole new meaning. It was something I always flashed back to as a manager when interviewing potential staff. Particularly when they would say, *I really love watching CSI on TV and it would be so interesting to work as a funeral director on those cases*. My first response always was, "It is not like TV, and fortunately it is not smell-a-vision".

CHAPTER THREE

Becoming the Manager

After a few years doing everything from the front desk to mortuary transfer, mortuary work, after-hours phone roster, then after-hours funeral arranger, funeral assistant, and funeral arranger conductor—I began to work towards the next level.

By becoming the manager of my own branch, the company had decided to go all out with in-house training of their staff. I completed a two-year course with the company, which included:

> *Certificate IV in Funeral Services*
>
> *Certificate IV in Training and Assessing*
>
> *Certificate IV in Frontline Management*

When I first applied for a manager's position, I did not get the job, based on how staff felt about me being in charge. The managers trialled me on the *Dale Carnegie Course*, which helped with my confidence. While doing the course, management approached me to stand in as acting manager, while the manager was on leave for a month. I soon learned there was another level to being in the manager's chair, as I worked out staffing issues for the day and coordination around transfer collections. I was doing the job to the best of my ability. Once the manager returned from holidays, I just went about my everyday work as before.

When our training manager returned from his long service leave, he was really ticked off that I had not been given a promotion. He took me aside and said quietly, "Today you are going to be offered two positions. One is second-in-charge at the Main Branch, and the other is manager of the Toowong Branch. I know it is a distance to travel every day to Toowong, but remember, it includes a company car and phone". He then told me he would really like to see me take on my own branch, as he had confidence in me to do the job well.

By the time the general manager approached me later that day, I had made up my mind to take the manager's position at Toowong.

I started working at the Toowong Branch on 1 January 2007. It was later that year, in October, that I returned to the crematorium where I started my career—as the manager. I had come full circle.

CHAPTER FOUR

Creating the Fond Farewell

Over the years I have worked with amazing families and have had them return to me to do another loved one's service. Whenever I sat with the family, I would talk about bringing memorabilia to the service to display the loved one's history.

Most families would stick to the one's photos or trophies from different sporting events, or their hat. However, more creative ways of honouring someone include:

The Surfer: A young man who had passed was an avid surfer, and his family used sand from his favourite surfing beach, his surfboard, and wet suit to honour him. They chose one of the *Expressions* coffins which was decorated with a beach scene. They then placed a tarpaulin on the floor beneath the coffin and spread beach sand and seashells on it to create the effect of the beach. The surfboard was placed on top of the coffin, and his wet suit hung on a stand behind the coffin in a position that looked like he was surfing. They placed single flowers on the beach sand during the service. They honoured his passion for surfing.

The Knitter: A woman who passed, knitted scarves for all her family. Each person in the family, which included her siblings and their children, her children, grandchildren, and great grandchildren, had all been given a special scarf she had knitted them. Instead of the standard flowers for the coffin, the family members all brought their scarves to the service. As they arrived, they placed them on the coffin—they looked amazing! At the end of the service, one-by-one, the family members went to the coffin and took their scarf back, and then exited the chapel. It was a very moving tribute that honoured the life of a daughter, sister, mother, grandmother, great grandmother, and aunt.

The Young Girl: A young girl, who had passed away from cancer, and her family had been gifted a trip to Walt Disney World through the *Make-A-Wish Foundation.* The family decorated around the coffin with all her favourite toys from Disney World and the Disney Castle. On the day of the service—to my amazement—I noticed there were folks dressed up as clowns. I was to find out later, they were doctors from the children's hospital who dressed up as 'Patch Adams' characters on the ward. Not knowing who Patch Adams was, my colleagues suggested that I see the movie *Patch Adams*, starring Robin Williams, and so I did. What a great principle! I take my hat off to the doctors and nurses who do this all the time for the kids.

The Welder: A father had died, and I was asked by his family if they could bring his welding machine to the service and place it near the coffin. My reply was, "Why not? As long as you put something under it, so not to scratch the floor". Then they told me the story of the welder: his sons and sons-in-law had been passing the welding machine amongst themselves for over ten years while the father had been in a nursing home. Every time they got together, Dad would ask, "Where is my bloody welder?" When it was brought to the service the boys carried it up to the coffin and said, "Sorry, we have taken our time, Dad—here is your welder." The humour and the tribute honouring the man's memory was wonderful.

The Gardener: This funeral was to honour the life of a gardener who did not like flowers. He had tolerated a small garden bed of flowers, which his wife looked after, but he had his own amazing garden filled with vegetables and fruit trees. So, instead of flowers, his children bought a box of fruit and vegetables to place on top of the coffin. How appropriate!

The RSL Poppy Service: There are many other ways to personalise a funeral, for instance, the RSL Poppy Service for our Veterans who have served in the Australian Defence Force and had active overseas service. The Poppy Service is conducted by a Member of an RSL Sub-Branch and is part of a funeral service. It is always nice when families acknowledge the service a person has made to our country.

Guards of Honour: Many sporting clubs like to honour their buddies with a guard of honour.

State Funerals: I have been involved with several state funerals. A state funeral is a public funeral ceremony, observing strict rules of protocol, held to honour people of national significance. My biggest one was for an Australian Federal Police officer. What an experience that was. The training and security that went into planning the funeral was phenomenal—just so it would be perfect on the day. Everything was checked and double-checked, and no stone was left unturned.

Taking the deceased home: Within the culture of the Samoan, Māori, and Tongan communities it is common to have their loved one at home, for some days, while family and friends gather and sit with the deceased prior to the funeral service. This practice, however, is not limited to a cultural aspect, and the funeral may also be held in the home of the deceased.

Let me share the story of a family and their choice of a *home funeral*. The funeral company I was working for was doing major advertising, and the catchphrase at that time was "We will do it your way". The family was trying to decide where to have the service, somewhere that was close to where they lived. I made arrangements to meet them at their house in Upper Brookfield to arrange the service. The family started to tell me how the deceased had never made it home. He had designed and built the house for his family, but he had become ill before the house was finished. He never lived in the house because he had spent his last six months in hospital.

While I was there, a feeling settled over me and I asked them how they felt about having the service at the house. The sons, who were from Melbourne, jumped right into the idea. It meant the family would not be restricted by the time allotted by a funeral home or crematorium chapel.

FOUR | Creating the Fond Farewell

They did not need to have a celebrant to run the service—they could do it all themselves.

On the day of the service, we took him home and the family and friends gathered around and just shared their memories with one another. When it was time to leave, they formed a guard of honour as we drove down the driveway. It gave me a *true* sense of creating a fond farewell.

The second home funeral I organised occurred when I returned to the crematorium as manager. I often drive past the little house in Deception Bay, and I am still amazed how we managed the funeral in that small backyard. It was what their Mum wanted. She was well known around Deception Bay for her charity work, and her family and friends created the fond farewell she deserved.

As the manager of a crematorium, I have seen many more ways families have honoured their family members. For instance, when the local car club lined their cars along the crematorium pathways as a guard of honour.

One particular family I had the honour of helping, asked to have their son's coffin bought into the crematorium chapel on the back of his ute. They took him from the chapel to the gravesite in the same way. The ute was his pride and joy—what better honour than to have him transported one last time in his precious vehicle? The family use the ute again when another member of the family passed away—it became a tradition.

Creating a Fond Farewell

Bike Clubs will have the captain lead the hearse to the chapel, while the members will follow on their bikes as it is arriving. After the service, the bike club will escort the hearse from the chapel to the gravesite.

One funeral company asked if the family could have their father's *working* steam engine parked outside the chapel during the service. It was the highlight of the day!

A well-known local man, who owned a trucking company, was honoured with all of his truck drivers parking their trucks along the road leading to the crematorium.

On one occasion, the local army base supplied a tank for the funeral one of its members.

Many families have organised dove releases or butterfly releases to follow the service. Balloon releases were also popular; however, they are not as common now due to new environmental rules and restrictions.

The list of options is endless. Over the years, I have suggested many different things for families to display to celebrate their loved one. If mum or dad had a garden, I would suggest that they bring flowers or cuttings from their garden, instead of buying flowers. For others, I would suggest having a candle lighting just before the beginning of the service. If the deceased had a hobby or was into music, it was okay to honour that by bringing in trophies or other related memorabilia. Children can be invited to draw pictures, or friends can be encouraged to write on the coffin, or even write a letter to their loved one to be placed into the coffin. As I say, the list is endless.

CHAPTER FIVE

Children Attending Funerals

One of the biggest questions I am often asked is whether children should attend the service. I have often replied by sharing with them a little about my history and how I found it very confusing not being allowed to go to a funeral. I would assure them it was their choice, and I recommended that they talk to the children to see how they felt about attending. Gone are the days when children should be seen and not heard.

I always think back to when I organised a funeral for a young boy of six who had passed from cancer.

> *I had never met him before he passed, but he left a big impact on my life. He had attended a funeral I had arranged, and told his parents he wanted me to be his funeral director. It was an honour, and I thank him for choosing me.*

This story shows how important it is that young children get to say goodbye.

I met the parents of the boy when they came to see me at the funeral home in Aspley. They rang and made an appointment with the company requesting they only spoke with me; they had been to a child's funeral I had organised and conducted a month or so before.

They sat and shared that their little boy was dying; he had terminal cancer. He had attended the funeral of a friend of his from the hospital. It had been held at the *Walkabout Creek* venue, nestled in the D'Aguilar National Park, overlooking the Enoggera Reservoir. I could not take credit for the venue, as it was a chosen by his parents. However, I digress—this story is different to his friend's funeral, but it is also entwined.

As he attended his friend's funeral, he turned to his parents and stated, "Mummy and Daddy, I am dying, and I want that lady to look after me". Wow! As the parents related this story I was completely blown away. When they approached me, I was extremely nervous as I was about to take annual leave. I let them know that, and then assured them other funeral directors within the company were more than capable to handle the funeral, if the sad event happened within the next few weeks.

It was about six months later when I met the parents again, after the little boy had passed. We sat to make the arrangements as to how the funeral was to run. They didn't want a funeral in the state forest, they did, however, want a Saturday service in their local church. A few phone calls later we had the time, date, and venue fixed.

Then we went on to talk about a viewing for the family on the night before the service. It was to be opened to extended family and friends for an hour in the chapel at Aspley. Because of the connection with the boy wanting me to look after him, I made sure I looked after the viewing as

FIVE | Children Attending Funerals

well as going to work on the Saturday, even though I was not rostered on. I felt, and believed, it was something I had to do for him.

On the night of the viewing as the family came and went, I stayed in the background keeping an eye on things and I watched a small boy several times approach his coffin. Every time he was stopped by his parents, I could see he was distressed. I approached the dad to assure him it was okay if he wanted to go up to the coffin. I was bluntly told, "No, we don't believe this would be good for him". My heart broke for the little one.

After everyone left, I put the coffin away and I spoke with him as I did and thanked him for this honour of looking after him. Even though we had not officially met in life he was now part of my spiritual family.

Next morning, I met with Nerida Thompson, who was my assistant at the funeral home, and we loaded the coffin into the hearse and headed off to the church. I filled Nerida in on what we were expected to do at the church, and she agreed it would be easier if she looked after the memorial book while I attended to the open coffin.

The family had invited anyone that had not already done so to come forward and write a message on the coffin. His mum insisted that I also place a message as I was now part of the family. I felt honoured. It was during this time as I stood beside his coffin and family and friends came and went, I noticed the same the little boy from the viewing the night before sneaking up to the coffin without his family seeing him. I had learned he was a cousin. As I was standing there, he made it to the coffin, he put his hand on his cousin's hand in the coffin, his little voice said, "I just wanted to say goodbye." His dad found him at the coffin. I said to his dad, "He just wants to say goodbye". Then his dad looked at me and nodded, so they both went back to the coffin to say their goodbyes.

As the funeral service at the church concluded, Nerida and I continued back to the funeral home while the family stayed to greet family and friends at the reception. After a quick bite of lunch and picking up the butterflies, Nerida and I got into the hearse and continued on to the crematorium to meet with the family for a private committal service. I had arranged for the butterflies to be delivered earlier that day so we could do a butterfly release at the crematorium. In my experience, once the butterflies are awake, they will gently fly away. But on this particular day one butterfly stayed with the family for half an hour and then it fluttered up into the trees and went on its way.

To this day, this is one of the special funerals that stays in my heart. *(I have not used names for reasons of privacy, however, I have told this story to illustrate sometimes we need to allow children to say goodbye in their own terms. Let's not place our fear of death in their hearts.)*

Over the years, I have found that children are far more resilient to death than some of us adults. I still remember a pretty little girl who was the apple of her father's eye. He sadly passed from cancer at a young age. On the day of the

FIVE | Children Attending Funerals

funeral, she went into the viewing and stood up on a chair and looked into the coffin and spoke to him as though he was asleep. She explained to him he was now going to be with the angels. She was only four. During the service many references were made to her being her father's princess and when the slide show started she got up and told us all that it was her with her daddy on the screen. Then she ran up to the coffin and said, "Goodbye daddy, have a nice time in heaven". What a lesson we could all learn from this. Her mother is to be commended for explaining to her daughter what death was.

I would like to share with you another instance where a child of a young age taught me a lot about saying goodbye.

I had the honour of conducting a funeral for a gentleman who had passed from cancer. I had met with him three times prior to his death, and as he put in place the things he wanted, he also pre-paid his funeral. Sadly, he passed a few days after all was in place; he was supported by his sister and her husband.

His sister and brother-in-law were gutted as they tried to come to terms with his passing. I spoke about their brother in a caring way and went through what he wanted to do for his service, and we spoke about how their grandchildren would react to his death. I shared with them the same advice I gave to everyone with young children. I told them to suggest they write him a letter or do a drawing for the deceased, as a special way of saying goodbye.

As we placed the coffin in the chapel, I opened the curtains so his two great-nieces could come forward with their drawings. I helped the girls place the pictures on display and asked the littlest one if she wanted to place the flowers near her drawing. Kids like to be involved, and she said, "Yes".

As the service drew to a close, I came forward to prepare the coffin to be carried out of the chapel when this youngest great-niece rushed forward with another drawing she had been busily working on during the service. It was a perfectly drawn heart just for her uncle she lovingly called Aussie.

As I was waiting at the hearse for all the mourners to come out of the chapel, she ran up to me excitedly to let me know Uncle Aussie was sleeping in the coffin and we had to be quiet so not to wake him. She told me how she talked on Skype with him all the time, but it's okay now because he is going to heaven, and she won't see him anymore on Nan's computer.

I assured her that her uncle was indeed going to heaven, and he was going to carry her special message with him.

As I led the hearse away, I could see her running amongst the mourners speaking with them about her uncle. I completed my tasks and had the family and friends gather in the refreshment lounge. I made my way back to my office, where another person waited for advice on what to do when their dad has passed.

FIVE | Children Attending Funerals

I returned to the refreshment lounge to say a final goodbye to the family. As I entered the room Little Miss made a beeline for me, and her next words blew me away. She asked in her matter-of-fact voice, "Is he in the oven yet?" With a smile on my face, I replied, "Yes", then we continued to have a matter-of-fact talk about Life and Death. She explained how her dog had just died, and so the conversation went on.

Over the years in my job, I have seen many sides to grief: I have seen the worst in people, and I have seen the best in people. The ones that blow me away most are the children and their uncanny way of being able to process the Life and Death experience far better than we adults. The Little Miss I referred to was four, she was such a joy and I felt very blessed to have met her.

When working with families with young children, I always suggest they allow the children to draw a picture and leave it with the deceased.

Whenever I have arranged a service for a baby born too soon, I like to suggest to the parents to write down their hopes and dreams for their child and place it in the coffin. They also might like to include a family photo to go with the child. If the parents have other young children, I like to suggest we get stickers so the children can decorate the coffin—it makes them feel part of the process. Sometimes they may even like to draw a picture on the coffin.

CHAPTER SIX

Some of my most memorable funerals

There have been many funerals over my 21 years of service in the funeral industry—here are a few that have been the most memorable.

The Little Ballerina

When the manager came into the arranger's office, she said to me, "I need you to go to a residence and bring a young girl into care, as she has passed away in the hospital overnight, and the parents have taken her home".

She instructed me to take a separate car as she wanted me to stay and arrange the funeral with the parents. The manager said her only hope was they hadn't put her in bed with an electric blanket. When I asked why, she replied with a sad face, "You will learn"—and that I did!

Upon arrival, I met with the family and, unfortunately, they had placed her in their bed with the electric blanket on because they didn't want her to feel cold. This was the very thing my manager had warned me about. I could tell the little body was too warm and decay was starting to happen. I sat with the family and spoke to them about what they wanted to do. My assistant and I then prepared to take their daughter into our care. When my assistant left, I stayed behind to go over what the parents wanted. They asked that she come back home until the service, so I contacted the office and we arranged for the embalmer to come in as soon as possible. I explained to her parents that when we bought her back home, she would need to be in an air-conditioned room, even though it was wintertime.

We worked on a timeline to bring her home. The parents had some ideas on how the service would go, but we decided to revisit these plans when we returned their daughter, the Little Ballerina, home.

When I got back to the office, I was met by the embalmer and he said, "All I can do is my best". She was already starting to break down. He worked on our ballerina for eight hours, just so we could take her home. He asked me to make sure the family would keep the room cold. Heat is not a good thing for a deceased body if you wish to have them at home until the time of the funeral.

The next day I rang the parents and arranged a time for me to take their Little Ballerina back to her home. I didn't need an assistant this time as dad was there to pick his daughter up in his arms.

We gently placed her in her bed, we made sure the air conditioner was set to low, and we put the fan on as well.

The celebrant arrived and we finalised plans for the funeral. Her parents had booked the *Walkabout Creek* venue to have the service in the forest area, followed by the wake in the restaurant. A private family service in the chapel at the crematorium was to follow later that day.

SIX | Some of my most memorable funerals

As I left the house, I double-checked on our Little Ballerina to make sure she was still okay. The plan was that I would come back each day, over the next three days, to check on her.

The next day I arrived at the house to be met by her mother, who was very distressed. She wanted us to take her baby into our care, but her father wasn't ready to part with her.

Upon entering the room, I could see why mum was distressed, and it took me another hour to sit with dad and explain what was happening. We eventually placed the Little Ballerina in our vehicle for me to take her into our care until the funeral on the Monday morning.

On the day of the funeral, it was beautiful and sunny as we carried the small coffin down the pathway. Her parents had arranged a 'fairy' to blow bubbles and sprinkle everyone with fairy dust, aka glitter.

As our ballerina had been embalmed, and we took her back into our care, we were able to have a brief open-coffin viewing. This was for all the children who had been in hospital with her, to come and say their final goodbyes. Being outdoors I made sure there was a viewing net placed over the coffin. A viewing net is a means used to soften the look of the deceased.

As the service came to a close the children released pink balloons. When we had the final committal service at the crematorium, I understood from watching the slide show why she was called *our ballerina*—she loved to put on her tutu and be a ballerina! *She is still dancing with the angels every day.*

Remembering Kiara Lee 'Wolfey' Pretsel

Born 28 December 2006 to Steven and Carissa Pretsel

One of the babies I cared for was the child of my hairdresser, Carissa. Carissa was so excited and had such wonderful plans for the baby when it would be born. As Carissa and her husband Steven didn't know the sex of the bub at the time, they lovingly referred to the baby as 'Wolfey'.

Carissa knew I had an intuitive side to me, and I could have a feeling about what sex the baby would be. When Carissa asked me what the sex of her baby might be, something held me back from saying anything. I told Carissa I did not want to spoil the surprise, and I sent up a silent prayer that my prediction would be wrong.

I can remember coming back to the office on a Friday afternoon—I had just been out on three transfers from the nursing home and hospitals that day. I checked in with the front desk, as I was to be the weekend arranger. I was told, "We have made you a residence appointment for a baby service, as we had no one here all day". The receptionist mentioned briefly that the mother knew me but, unfortunately, she only gave me the surname of the person and it was not one I recognised. I actually didn't know Carissa's surname; she was only known to me as 'Carissa who was my hairdresser'. As it was knock-off time, I didn't put a lot of stock in trying to figure out who it was. I

SIX | Some of my most memorable funerals

collected my bag, put the address in my notebook and headed home. The next morning, I headed off for the day.

As I pulled up at the address, a strange feeling came over me—I had a *knowing*. As I got out of the car, (still not knowing the full name of the mum) Carissa's face popped into my head. I started to walk towards the steps and the front door flew open and there stood Carissa. I was devastated. She said, "I bet you weren't expecting to see me today", and then she looked into my face and said, "You knew. That's why you didn't want to tell me the sex of the baby".

I have often wondered why the universe had chosen me to be in the profession into which I had fallen. This was one of those times I really questioned the judgement. The funeral service date and time was set, and it ended with a balloon release at the crematorium.

As a funeral director I never expect to become friends with families, most families really don't want to talk to you again, unless it is to arrange another service for the family. I am extremely fortunate that Carissa and Steven are such wonderful people, and they remain my friends to this day. If I run into Carissa when I'm out and about, she will always introduce me as 'Wolfey's' funeral director. For this I am forever grateful.

It was also my honour to be the funeral director when Carissa's mum passed away, even though I was now employed with another funeral company.

From Carissa and Steven Pretsel

Rita-Marie has been our funeral director twice. The first time was for our daughter in January 2007, and the second time was for my Mum in March 2017.

Rita-Marie was always professional and compassionate. She made us feel that we were heard, and she communicated clearly with us, which I believe is so important for a funeral director.

I had known Rita-Marie for a little while, previously to our daughter's funeral, because I was her hairdresser.

After the way she handled our daughter's funeral we knew she was who we wanted when my Mum passed away.

I don't believe this job is for the faint-hearted.

Remembering Craig Springsteen

3 October 2007

Suicide has touched me closely on many occasions. When the word came that one of our own, Trish Springsteen, had lost her son Craig in this way, it touched all of the staff at the funeral home. I knew who Trish was; she was the former manager of the crematorium where I had started my career, and I had met Trish once or twice over the years.

Trish arranged the service via our branch manager, Nerida Thompson, from our Redcliffe office. As I was the after-hours arranger, it was my job to look after the viewing for Craig's friends, to be held the night before the service.

SIX | Some of my most memorable funerals

My job that night was to set Craig up in the chapel and be on-hand while his friends came to say their private farewell. What was to be an hour-long viewing turned into three hours. Trish and her family had a private family viewing earlier in the day, so in the evening, Trish's husband, Peter, and her sister Jacquie were on hand to greet Craig's friends.

When Craig's friends arrived, they sat outside of the chapel for the first 30 minutes, speaking in hushed tones, berating themselves for not noticing the struggles Craig had. As time passed, gradually, they went inside one-by-one and paid their respects. The resounding comments I heard time and time again, was how sorry they were that they had let Craig down.

I felt honoured to be able to help Trish's family and friends through this time. The hardest part of the night for me was letting everyone know it was time for them to leave. Over the years since then, Trish and I have become close friends. We share a common bond, as I went on to become the manager of the crematorium where Trish served all those years ago, and it is now Craig's forever home.

It is always Trish's hope that, through her stories, we will continue to remember Craig. Even today when I visit the crematorium where I once managed, I will always pop by and say hello to him.

Remembering the life of Julie McColl

For the period between 24 and 26 March 2003

Julie McColl was the first murder victim, that I had ever looked after. Julie was the second, and last, victim of the infamous murders of sex workers that took place in Brisbane between 2002 and 2003. The irony of looking after Julie's funeral was not lost on me, as I had driven past the first *sex worker murder* site on the day a member of the public had found the victim.

I can remember saying to my friend, who was in the car with me, that someone must have been deceased as I had recognised the Coroner's Funeral Directors waiting at the site. It was a shock when I watched the news that evening to realise that we had driven past a murder scene.

When Julie McColl's body was found, her family came to arrange the service to be held in the chapel of the crematorium where I worked. I was honoured to be the person to organise a fond farewell for someone who'd had a tough life. It was clear that she was loved by her family, and they wanted to acknowledge the person she was before she fell on hard times. This taught me, no matter what a person has done, there is always a family who loves them.

Arrangements were made so her partner, who was in prison, could attend. Her friends and colleagues also attended the service. There was a young man who spoke about how Julie had saved his life. What I wasn't prepared

SIX | Some of my most memorable funerals

for was the media coverage and how disrespectful they were in their treatment of her.

The family had agreed to media interviews at their home and even invited the media to attend the wake—but they respectfully asked them not to attend the funeral service. Despite this request there was a film crew, with zoom lenses, that positioned themselves in the car park. I saw myself on the television news that night giving the cameraman my most peeved-off expression!

There was also a news reporter in the chapel who then wrote a piece in the newspaper that tried to make Julie sound *less* than she was. It criticised the family for remembering only Julie's good points, even though—during the eulogy—the family had acknowledged her hard times, without making mention of what she did for a living. Julie was born in New Zealand, and in her native country they paid tribute to her life in the local newspaper.

A link to the article appears below.

https://www.nzherald.co.nz/nz/mourners-illustrate-double-life/U5O46DY54XCDQIUTYFHNHB5BGY/

You can view the story of the arrest of Julie's murderer via the following link.

From life saver to serial killer
https://cdn.newsapi.com.au/link/7afe5f04dac82e1122dff79f135d1ca3?domain=couriermail.com.au

Remembering Adam Sager

19 March 1982 to 29 April 2007

At the age of 24, Adam was a fit and healthy young man. He was training for the martial arts world championships when he first developed symptoms of the asbestos disease, mesothelioma. Adam died just ten months later at 25 years of age.

As mentioned previously, I was the manager at a funeral branch in Toowong, and the funeral company at that time was advertising "We will do it your way". This promotion was targeted at the younger generation, and one of the advertisements showed a burly man with tattoos all over his body. On the morning after Adam had passed, I arrived at the office to find that I had a message to contact his parents. I made the phone call and spoke with Adam's mum, Julie, and agreed to meet her at Adam's residence to make the funeral arrangements. Julie sounded so tired, but she wanted to get the arrangements underway at the house. As I sat with Adam's parents Julie and Don, and Adam's sister Tegan and her partner Conlan, they started telling me about Adam. How he loved martial arts, and his work with kids. Adam had a dream to create a space where kids could have a good time and be safe. They fondly told me what he was like as a youngster, and about how he loved to help his parents when they were building their first home in Townsville. As they talked, Adam's spirit started to make himself known to me, I could sense he was in the

SIX | Some of my most memorable funerals

room: I have a spot on my back that alerts me to spirit every time.

Now this was not something I talked about very often, as I didn't want people to think I was *nuts*. So, in my usual fashion, I acknowledged quietly to myself that his spirit was there, but I didn't say anything to the family at that point. Adam kept poking at me. Julie recalls I had a twitch, which she thought was strange. When we were starting to talk about celebrants, Adam's spiritual healer, Bruce, arrived to pay his respects to the family and offer his help!

Bruce and the family spoke about Adam and his spirituality. Bruce mentioned that Adam was with everyone and sitting beside Julie, he then turned to me and said, "You are also intuitive". Well! At this point Adam would not stay quiet. I had to come clean, and I had to let them know Adam was indeed with them. We talked for a while about Adam and what he wanted to say, and the intuitive side of my character.

It was decided that I would be the MC for the day and allow Adam to channel through me to run the funeral service. I agreed, and then I started to get back to the arrangements, Julie said, "Really, do we need to discuss this now?" I nodded and said, "Yes, we do". We started to discuss choices of coffins. Tegan said the coffin had to be black, Adam's favourite colour. The family shared how they wanted to put a logo from Adam's business brand on the top of the coffin. At this point they realised Adam was driving the arrangements. We decided to hold the service in the chapel of a crematorium close to Toowong.

Adam was saying to me, "No, not a church". I had to assure Adam it was peaceful, and it wasn't a church, and that it had kangaroos and nature all around it. He then agreed, "Okay". As we were coming to the end of making the arrangements, I asked them, "What made you choose our company?" They replied that the first reason was locality, as my branch was just around the corner from where Adam lived. The second reason was the advertisements with the tattooed man. Julie expressed that she was a little disappointed I didn't have tattoos—but knowing I was an intuitive person was just as good.

When I returned to work, I consulted my boss to make sure he was happy with the idea. We were doing it their way. Then I needed to choose an assistant who totally understood who I was and what I was about to do. Enter the lovely Annette Lourigan, our branch manager from Springwood, at that time. She was the one person in the company I knew would understand. Annette and I had worked together on projects throughout our careers, and she was the only person that I trusted would not be freaked out about what I was about to try. Annette was aware of my spirituality; she had seen it a few times before and she was also what we refer to as an *empathic soul*. Annette agreed to be the assistant on the day of the funeral, and then went one step further and contacted the main branch to request that she would collect Adam. She also helped with dressing him in the mortuary. On the day, Annette

SIX | Some of my most memorable funerals

drove Adam to the service. We set him up in the viewing room and when the family arrived, they placed the transfer of Adam's business brand onto the lid of the coffin.

As I was taking the coffin into the chapel from the viewing room, Annette entered the chapel and approached Julie, who was sitting in the front row gathering her thoughts. Annette said, "I don't know why, but I was asked to pick this flower for you". She presented Julie with a yellow rose and Julie told Annette that she knew why. The service was about to begin; the family had put together a list of people who would speak, and in what order, and a CD with a list of Adam's favourite songs.

I was to take my cue from Adam when he would want the music to start and stop. At the start of the service, I introduced myself and explained, "I may seem strange and come out with some really weird statements, but don't worry as it means Adam is with us". I started introducing the speakers and then Adam would tell me it was time to play another tune. It was in one such moment when I asked Annette to play the next song. Well, the song *Chop Suey* by 'System of a Down' began to play, and I started nodding my head along to the music—it was a song Adam was really into.

There is a line in the song that I thought said, "Angels deserve to fly". No! The line was, "I ... cry ... when angels deserve to die". Something made me look at Julie, Don, and Tegan. At first, they looked shocked, and then they started laughing. I looked at Annette and the look on her face was

51

one of pure horror, she keep signalling that the song needed to end; however, Adam had other ideas—he wanted the song to play out, so we let it go.

After the service, Annette told me why she wanted to stop the song and then I understood why she had that look of horror on her face. Speaking with Julie and Don later, I learnt they had cut that song from the list the night before as they didn't think it was appropriate, even though Adam often played that song. Conlan and Tegan put the CD together and chose the tracks and, to this day, they still do not know how that song ended up on it.

It is my belief, and experience, that spirit has a way of getting around things. Adam wanted the song to be played as it was his way of letting the family know he was really there, and it was his way of saying goodbye. Adam became a big part of who I was, as a funeral director. While I often receive messages from the *beyond*, Adam was the only spirit I have willingly allowed to totally take over my body to act through me. I did find the experience draining. Anyone who works on the physic plane will tell you it takes a lot of energy from you.

I still keep a close contact with Julie, sometimes in person, but usually via social media. Julie and Don Sager did not let Adam's memory fade with the funeral—they went on to become strong advocates and educators about the risk of working with asbestos, especially for do-it-yourself renovators.

SIX | Some of my most memorable funerals

From the Sager Family

What do you say to someone who changed your life, like you did for our family, Rita-Marie? On the day we first met you, we had no idea where we were headed and how this 'moment' was going to evolve. Having never experienced the death of a child, let along one of our own, you were the glue, the one constant. You, with the help of our Adam, walked us through the process of the funeral whilst providing safe passage into and through our grief.

It has been 15years since this time and you still catch us as we teeter and wobble our way through the same grief.

Your attention to detail was mixed with compassion and understanding, also knowing you had to complete your mission. Although it was not part of your usual job description you agreed to conduct the service for Adam's Farewell. Gee weren't there some funny goings on? You managed them, and us, seamlessly and made it as pain-free as possible whilst keeping your composure—even while THAT song played when it was not supposed to. We still chuckle about that.

We cannot thank you enough for just being you (for your little messages from Adam) … you will always be part of us. You are always that constant inspiration.

With Love … Julie, Don, Tegan and Conlan

You can find more about Adam on YouTube at

"Losing Breath" – The Adam Sager Story.

https://www.youtube.com/watch?v=Fqk5FDm1i-Q

CHAPTER SEVEN

Being an intuitive and empathic individual

I could not have shared Kiara's, Julie's, or Adam's stories without touching on the intuitive and empathic side of my nature. Every funeral director I know has that side to them; it is what makes them good funeral directors.

I learnt at a young age that I had an intuitive side to my nature—it was something that had been passed down to me by my mother. My mother had an uncanny way of *knowing* when someone close to our family was going to pass away.

I still remember the morning she said to my stepfather, "We need to go home to Winton, I dreamt I was attending Aunty Alice's funeral last night". Our family was living in a Main Roads camp between Isisford and Ilfracombe in outback Queensland, at the time. My stepfather told my mother to stop being stupid, but that weekend when we went into Ilfracombe for our normal week's shopping the police officer met Mum at the post office. As my mother looked at him, she said, "Alice has died, hasn't she?" We arrived home in Winton just as the funeral began, and just as my mother had predicted.

She did exactly the same thing when my great-grandmother had passed, and also with our grandad. I got used to feeling things as a young child; a simple *knowing* would come over me and I would see things as they were about to happen. So, for me being in tune with the spirit world was pretty normal—not that I shared it with anyone, I didn't want people to think I was completely nuts!

Over the years I have had experiences as described earlier, however, there are two other incidents that gave me pause for thought in my final years as a funeral director.

In the first instance, the television news ran a story that a young man had been shot at his house in our local community. As the new flash was starting, I said to my husband, "I will do his funeral". Luckily for me, my husband is used to me coming out with strange things like this. It never ceases to amaze me how the universe will connect me with families that I have a bond with in some way. In the case of this young man, he was the nephew of a family friend, who had relatives in our hometown of Winton, and they would holiday out there often. Mum's friend would tell me about the times he danced with my mother at the old-time dances.

In the months leading up to this event, I had arranged a funeral for a lady who was well known back in Winton. At the service, an old family friend was in attendance; he knew the family well, and he was distantly related to the deceased son-in-law.

At some time later there was a funeral for a young girl that I had been requested to arrange. However, due to other commitments, I handed over the arrangements to my assistant. Not only did I know the parents and grandparents

SEVEN | Being an intuitive and empathic individual

of the young girl, but I had also gone to school with one of her aunts. Then, I realised the girl was the great-niece of our old family friend; I said to him on the day of the funeral, "We must stop meeting like this".

When it came time to do his nephew's funeral, I just shook my head and understood why I knew I would be arranging the funeral. I have learnt not to question my intuitive side, although there are times when I just wish it would stop.

The next time I had this same feeling about organising a funeral was for a small boy of three years of age. I was at my doctor's surgery when a little one—very distressed and visibly in pain—came out of the doctor's office. His dad took him outside while mum paid the account and arranged a follow-up appointment. It was plain to see he wasn't well; I went into the chemist next door, and when dad and the little fellow came into the chemist behind me, I could see he wasn't in a happy place. I still see him as he stopped crying and looked at me with his big eyes, and I knew in that moment he was going to be the next child I arranged a service for—it happened two months later.

The universe has given me such wonderful experiences during my time as a funeral director, I have always felt honoured to be part of a celebration of life.

CHAPTER EIGHT

Being the funeral director *and* the celebrant

There are some companies that offer to be a funeral celebrant as part of the service they provide to the families. This is usually a cost-effective way to do things and there is nothing wrong with that service. As a funeral director myself, it was never something I wanted to do, as they are two completely different roles.

I have, however, stepped up at least five times in my career to become the celebrant as well as the funeral director, when necessary. The first time was for my dear friend's mother. It was my way of helping her keep the cost of the service down, and it was my honour to be able to support her at that time.

The next time was when we had finished a funeral service at a church, and we (the funeral directors) were to go on alone to the graveside for a non-attended committal. On our way to the cemetery that intuitive side (that little voice that often pops into my head) said that we should perform a brief committal service graveside. I always carried in my folder a go-to quick-guide for a semi-religious service, if needed. This particular day as we placed the coffin, I offered the words of the committal placing of Symbolic Sand and lowered the coffin while we bowed our heads and took our hats off. When this was finished, the 'boys' (my funeral assistants) said, "Hey, we have an audience". I had thought the people nearby were just visiting another grave in the cemetery.

It turns out my angels were working well with me that day, as they were family members of the deceased, and they had missed the church service. When they heard there would be no one at the graveside they decided to come along, but stay in the distance. By the time we were back in the office they had already called through and thanked our company for the wonderful care we had taken; it was not something they expected us to do. Normally for a non-attendance committal we would be reverent and inter the coffin, but we never spoke. However, on that day a calling came that I should—so I did.

The next time I crossed into being a celebrant was for an Australian gentleman who had passed. His wife was from Korea, and she did not like the idea of a cremation service— she wanted him buried. However, since money was a problem, the only recourse for her was a *government-assisted funeral* which gave two options: a cremation service, or a burial in a government-assisted plot with someone not related to him.

After some discussion with her daughter, who lived in Korea, it was agreed she would continue with the *service* that had been arranged at the crematorium for all of his friends. And the daughter agreed to pay for him to be *buried* the next day in the Toowong Cemetery with no one in attendance, only his wife.

EIGHT | Being the funeral director *and* the celebrant

Toowong Cemetery is one of the oldest cemeteries in the city of Brisbane, it is set on a hillside with an incredible view of the city. The cemetery has many rows on the hillside and the valleys, throughout. We were lucky to find they had a gravesite available that hadn't been sold, however, it was in the valley of the cemetery, and we had to carry the coffin a fair way down the hill from the roadside. Thinking back, on that day, we must have looked comical as the three of us struggled carrying the coffin down the hill, taking small breaks along the way, while the wife continued running around us, filming with her video camera on us all the way down the hill. When we finally arrived at the gravesite, red-faced and exhausted, we set the coffin up. His wife decided she wanted me to perform a bit of a service with some prayers leading up to the committal, all the while training the camera on me and speaking in Korean. It is nice to know I am memorialised on a video somewhere in Korea. I am forever grateful that I had my little booklet in my folder that day!

As mentioned in Chapter Six, I was the stand-in celebrant for Adam Sager's funeral service.

When I was working as the crematorium manager, one of the first funerals I had arranged was a service for a lady whose family were estranged, and she was living in a *de facto* relationship. They wanted a funeral service for people to attend, but didn't want a celebrant, they just wanted me to do it.

Well, that is possible—except for one thing! No one would part with any memories of who she was. All I could gather was her date of birth, where she was born, and when and where she was married. I also had her children's names, but that was the extent of the details. I did some creative searching on Google about the day she was born and found she shared the same birthday as Billy Joel. I talked about the changing world at that time and tried my best to have someone come forward to say something about her. The silence was deafening and uncomfortable, to say the least.

I take my hat off to each and every funeral celebrant who, when they find themselves in this position, have to use their creativity to give someone an honourable farewell.

The last time I stepped forward was when a celebrant was unable to make the service; he was delayed, due to a traffic accident. As a funeral director, we are always prepared for such a scenario and, as luck would have it, this celebrant always sent me through the script for the service. This allowed the service to go ahead without any hiccups, and the family was extremely grateful. So was the celebrant I substituted for!

CHAPTER NINE

Funerals in the time of COVID-19

In the final 18 months of my career as a funeral director and manager of the crematorium, COVID-19 had come to our shores. At first, in the January of 2020, I wasn't overly concerned; this was to be another virus that the country prepared for by putting protocols in place. In my career, I experienced the Bird flu, the Swine flu, Creutzfeldt – Jakob Disease (CJD), SARS, and many more.

Funeral companies always have strict infection control protocols around dealing with the deceased. The two companies I had worked for always made sure our funeral directors were up-to-date with their immunisations. It was policy for us to have the influenza injection yearly, especially because aged care facilities insisted on proof-of-vaccination before we were allowed to collect the deceased.

Moving into February of 2020, things were starting to become real, and panic was starting to set in around the country. Then, in March 2020, came the mandates that were to continue over the next few years.

I was to arrange the funeral of a young teenager who was murdered in our local skate park. Due to the circumstances that surrounded his death, we could not have a service immediately because we had to wait for the coroner to release him. As the day of the funeral service drew near it became clear the government was putting strict restrictions in place. We had to start wearing masks, we were not allowed to shake hands, we had to stand 1.5 metres away from our clients, we couldn't have any more than two people at a time in the office, funeral numbers were cut down, and every day more things changed.

On the day of the service, what was potentially a funeral that would have had over four hundred mourners, it came down to only eight family members, as well as the two funeral staff members and celebrant, who were allowed to be at the service. There were two police officers in attendance outside the chapel to make sure no additional people came. Our crematorium had been proactive for a number of years with providing families a live streaming service. So, we were able to set up the live stream for folks to tune in and watch the service at home—it was a different way to be part of the service.

I was not allowed to hug the parents, and anyone who knows me will know how hard that was for me. It is my natural instinct to hug a grieving mother, father, child, etc. It felt so cold, so impersonal; the parents were so angry and so sad. As an empathic person I felt every emotion they were feeling, it was cutting into me like a knife. It was hard enough for the family having to have the funeral under such tragic circumstances, without having such harsh restrictions placed upon them.

NINE | Funerals in the time of COVID-19

This was the beginning of the end for me. On that day, after the service had finished, my staff tried to comfort me. They gave me space, as I tried to make it through the rest of the day. I came home to my family and, for the first time in my years as a funeral director, I completely broke down and sobbed. It was horrible, I felt so bad that I could not give the family their fond farewell for their son.

As the months progressed, the face of funerals changed: families were starting to look at non-attended cremations. And for the services which did go ahead, many families would still try to bargain with how many people could attend the service. I was immensely grateful we had the live streaming service that mourners could log onto.

The staff became targets as they had to monitor how many people would be in the grounds, but we needed to stick to the government mandates. I became the barrier that stood between my staff and the angry, grieving families. We had to place restrictions on how many people could visit our facility, and my job was to protect the company and my staff.

As the manager, it was my job to ensure other funeral companies stuck to the protocols that were in place, especially making sure they kept their numbers to what was allowed. As funeral directors and crematorium staff, we didn't get to work from home— we turned up for work every day. People were still passing away, and cremations and burials still had to go ahead.

I became hardened, which made me seem uncaring and cold. It was getting harder and harder each day for me to get up and go into work. I had lost my passion.

So, it was in June of 2021 that I decided I needed to have a couple of days off—that turned into three weeks while my husband recovered from an operation. I was sitting at home, watching him struggle, and thought *what am I doing?* It was in that moment I made a decision about my future, and said, "That is it, I am finishing!" Upon my arrival back at work, I sat down and emailed the company directors to give them three months' notice.

Leading up to my retirement, funeral numbers had started to increase, which allowed more people to attend services. We still had to have protocols around how many could sit in the chapel, and how many could be outside. Then we had to introduce the Check-In app, "Oh what fun!" says I, with tongue-in-cheek.

Funeral attendance numbers went up and down like a yo-yo, and just when I thought I was starting to feel okay about arranging funerals—bam, I was arranging a service for another person who had been murdered in Brisbane. I knew the person's mother and she was comfortable with me as the arranger. At the time of making the arrangements, we were allowed up to 100 people to attend a service. The Queensland Government was now opening the borders to New South Wales, which was helpful, as the deceased's brother had come from New South Wales to help with the arrangements. Once again, we had to wait for

NINE | Funerals in the time of COVID-19

the coroner to release the body for the service. But then, you guessed it, the government introduced new numbers of attendance: overnight it went from 100 to 80, and by the end of the week it was down to 30. Then on the day of the service we were only allowed 20. Once again, I had to turn people away and deal with the anger of mourners. That day I railed at God and said, "How could you be so cruel?" I was glad the end of my career was approaching.

So, on 30 September 2021, after 21years I closed the door on my funeral director's career. I always say the Universe/God has a plan for our lives, and I am eternally grateful I had the career I had—it has led me onto something better. Yes! I am still looking after families, but now as I do it as the Celebrant: it allows me to continue with the work that I love, and I have time to hug my grandbabies, look after my family, and catch up with my friends.

Over the years, I have learnt that people may not remember your name, but they will always remember how you made them feel. I wasn't always perfect, and I did have my moments. However, I would like to think that I have left the families that I served with a feeling of contentment, that they remembered their loved one, and celebrated their life by creating a *Fond Farewell*.

CHAPTER TEN

Organising the Funeral Service.

One thing I would like to say to anyone arranging a funeral is: *don't rush into the service.* Choosing your funeral director is one of the most fundamental parts of any funeral arrangement. You don't need to settle on the first one you call, you have time to decide. Unless, of course, your loved one already has things in place with a funeral company of their choosing.

Bear in mind, if a funeral director says they are unable to have your service on a certain day, it is because the chapel may be booked out, or they have many more funerals already booked on that day. So, the things you need to think about when speaking with the funeral director are things, such as:

1. When would you like to have the service?
2. Which venue is the service to take place in?
3. Will it be for burial or cremation?
4. Will you want to have a viewing?
5. Will you have a slide-show presentation of photographic memories?
6. Do you want the funeral company to provide this for you, or is a member of the family going to?

7. What music would you like played during the service?
8. Is it to be a religious or non-religious service?
9. What clothes do you want the deceased to wear? Are they going to wear their own clothing, or do you want the funeral director to supply a shroud?
10. Will there be any jewellery left on the deceased or do you want it returned?
11. Do you want the pallbearers to carry the coffin into or out of the church/chapel or onto the grave?
12. Do you have pallbearers, or do you want the funeral director to supply them?
13. Do you want a funeral notice in the papers?
14. Do you want flowers for the casket? If so, do you want the funeral company to provide them?

Bear all of this in mind when you meet with your funeral director, because every element takes time to organise. When the funeral director gives you a timeline to supply any of the items, they do so for a reason. They need to stick to strict timelines to make sure that everything runs smoothly on the day.

As a funeral director, I was often looking after several families all at once. And before I met with any family, I would try to gauge just when we could fit the service in— keeping in mind the family's needs as well. I often would share with a family, if they were rushing to *just get it over*

TEN | Organising the Funeral Service

with, my story of my mother's funeral service. I would remind them that I couldn't just go back and dig her up and do it over again. So, take the time and sit in remembrance of your loved one to honour them and celebrate their life.

As the family, you are only dealing with one funeral at that time. However, your funeral directors may be dealing with three, or more, on any given day.

Having a funeral service for the deceased is a way to honour their lives, and it gives the family and friends a time to grieve. When I sit with families, and they tell me that mum or dad didn't want a fuss, I understand that—especially if the family are at loggerheads. But the funeral isn't just for the person in the coffin; it is also for the ones left behind so they themselves have closure.

I sat with families riddled with guilt because they had fallen out with the deceased. I sat with families who were grieving so hard it made them angry that the loved one had gone. I have learnt over the years that, no matter what I feel, I have to remain calm and help them create that fond farewell they want—and to be there for them in that moment.

Once the service was over, most people would come up to me and say, "Thank you for a lovely service, and don't take this the wrong way, but I hope we never see you again". All I could ever do was smile and say, "Hey! I do live in your local area, so if you see me around, say 'hello', I don't bite." I learnt not to take this too personally, I found most families gave me a smile if they saw me in public. Very few would turn and run the other way.

CHAPTER ELEVEN

Funerals: *Attended or Non-attended*

Whether the family decides to have a funeral service, or a non-attended service, is up to them; they can still create a fond farewell with whatever form they choose. Funeral services can take place in a church, crematorium chapel, the family home, in their favourite park, at the graveside or or—with special permission—at sea.

Attended service
An *attended* funeral is one where the funeral service is held with the coffin present, and with family members and mourners in attendance. A *memorial service* is similar, however, there is no coffin present. Both may be held at any venue of the family's choice.

Non-attended service
A *non-attended* funeral is one where the deceased is delivered directly to the crematorium or cemetery by the funeral director, and no family attend. If it is by cremation the ashes can be collected, and the family may choose to: have a memorial service at their church at a later date; or memorialise the ashes at a crematorium or cemetery; or have a scattering of the ashes in a place meaningful to the family so they can bid a final farewell. This allows families to say goodbye in their own way and have closure. With a non-attended burial there is always a permanent memorial

place for the family to visit at their leisure. I know for myself it was a place I always went to when I wanted to be close to my great-grandmother. If I was in trouble at home, you could be guaranteed to find me sitting at her graveside.

When you first contact the funeral company

When someone passes you are, most likely, in shock and you may feel overwhelmed—don't worry this is quite normal. Here are some things to consider:

1. If your loved one has passed away in the hospital, they are taken to the hospital morgue. The family has time to go home, rest, and think about which funeral company they wish to use, and to contact them.

2. If they have passed away at home and in a palliative care situation, your loved one will be under the care of the palliative care team. You then let them know of your loved one's passing and, once they have attended to the deceased and issued either a *life extinct* or *death* certificate, you may then contact the funeral company of your choice. You don't have to rush to do this in the middle of the night. If you are comfortable to sit with your loved, one keep the room cool, and allow the family to spend time with them before the funeral director arrives.

3. If your loved one has passed away at home without warning, you will need to call the emergency number—in Australia this is 000. If you call for the ambulance, they will contact the police for you.

ELEVEN | Funerals: *Attended or Non-attended*

4. The police will take steps to speak with the family doctor to check if the deceased had any health issues. If the doctor is uncertain, or the deceased has not seen a doctor in over three months, then the police will call the government-appointed funeral director to take the deceased to the coroner.

5. Should the family doctor come to the residence and issue a life extinct or death certificate, then the family may go ahead and choose a funeral company to take their loved one into care.

6. When you contact the funeral director they will ask you a few questions—for example: the name of the deceased; the location where they passed away; the deceased's home address; the deceased's birthdate; and details of the doctor who will be issuing the Form Nine. (A Form Nine is a Medical Cause of Death Certificate)

7. Other information that will be helpful for the funeral director—especially if it is a home transfer—is to advise the *exact* location of the deceased; if there are any stairs they will have to navigate; and if the deceased is a large person. All of this information helps the company when they send their staff to the residence.

CHAPTER TWELVE

Burial or Cremation

Working at a crematorium, you soon learn that there are two options for families: burial or cremation. When my mother passed, my family chose a burial. It was what folks in small country towns did because there were no local crematoriums. Crematoriums are generally located in large cities.

The first time I heard of cremation was when I saw a movie that had been set in India. The movie touched on the Hindu tradition of cremation, and their belief that the deceased person was later reincarnated as an animal. In this particular movie the woman's ashes were spread out to sea and the closing scene had a white dove settling on the bow of the boat. That was it! I was sold on the idea of cremation—coming back as a dove was very appealing to a young girl.

The next day in school I told my teacher, Sister Mary Magdalene, about the movie and how I was going to be cremated, as you come back as a dove. Well, that led to the nun telling me she would have to pray for my soul for the rest of eternity. In those days Catholics did not believe in cremation; it is something that has changed for the better now.

However, I digress. When someone dies, families have options open to them. The first thing they need to decide is *what would the deceased have wanted*—if they have not left the family clear instructions.

A funeral director needs to know these preferences, as they have to to prepare the legal documentation according to them. In the case of a cremation there are additional forms and processes that have to be completed.

Understanding Cremation documentation

1. **Form 1, 'Application for permission to cremate'.** *Side note—the person who signs the Form One is the **only** person who can collect the ashes from the crematorium—unless they have given clear instructions in writing for another person to collect. This is one of the most emotional things for crematorium staff to deal with: when a funeral director has not clearly explained the process at the time of the arrangements.*

2. The questions on the Form 1 are to be answered by the applicant or person in charge of arranging the funeral, for example: a family member, or executor to the deceased estate. In some cases, it is the funeral company on behalf of the above persons, who have signed an authority for the funeral director to act on their behalf. ***This form is a legal requirement.***

3. **Form 4, 'Permission to Cremate'.** The funeral director will use the Form 1 to apply for the Form 4,

TWELVE | Burial or Cremation

'Permission to Cremate'. This is supplied by an independent doctor or the coroner.

4. **'Application for the Death Certificate'** form. This form gathers information required by Births, Deaths and Marriages to register the person's death. You will be asked for the family history of the person:

    - Full name and address of the deceased.
    - Where they were born.
    - Date of birth, and date of death, and their current age.
    - What was their occupation?
    - Were they born overseas and, if so, what year did they arrive in Australia?
    - In Australia—are they of Aboriginal or Torres Strait Islander descent?
    - Were they married, *de facto*, divorced, separated, never married or widowed?
    - Where they were married, how old they were, and to whom they were married. *(It is important to note that, if they have been married more than once, all marriages are to be recorded. If the information is not known to you, it is best to state 'unknown'.)*
    - The full names and occupations of their parents, especially the mother's maiden name.
    - If they have children, their names, and dates of birth, including children who are deceased. *(You can only record the names of their birth*

children or their legally adopted children. If there are children from a partner's marriage, and they were not adopted by the deceased, they cannot be listed as their children.)
- The funeral director will complete where the service was held, on what day, and who the priest/celebrant was.
- This form, along with the **'Form 9 Medical Cause of Death Certificate',** is sent to Births, Deaths, and Marriages the day after the funeral, cremation, or burial takes place.

5. Should the deceased have passed away in the hospital, or they are at the Coroner's Office, you will need to fill in a statement giving the funeral company permission to collect the person from the facility.

6. The funeral director will contact the deceased's doctor or hospital, or the Coroner's Office, to obtain the 'Form 9 Medical Cause of Death Certificate' or 'Coroner's Release'. *(This is **not** the official death certificate.)* This certificate, or coroner's release, is required by law, and the original will be sent to Births, Deaths, and Marriages along with the Death Certificate Application form. Births Deaths and Marriages will then produce the official death certificate to be sent to the family.

7. You need to think about how long you wish the crematorium to hold onto the ashes. Under the **Cremations Act 2003**, the crematorium has the right

TWELVE | Burial or Cremation

to dispose of the ashes after 12 months. They must give notice to the applicant in writing; if there is no reply within a 28-day period they can dispose of the ashes. As the manager of the crematorium, I did not dispose of the ashes in the 12-month period, unless I was instructed in writing to do so by the applicant. It was our company policy to always try to contact the family for up to five years before we would make that decision. Each crematorium has their own policies and procedures, which must align to the *Cremations Act 2003*.

8. Remember, not everything you wish to place with the deceased in the coffin can be cremated. It is best to speak with the funeral director or the crematorium on what is allowed. Also, give some thought to the clothing you want your loved one dressed in, as some materials are not acceptable for cremating. Once again, check with the funeral director or crematorium about this.

9. I have often been asked to place a loved one's pet's ashes, or another deceased's ashes, into the coffin with the deceased. I always recommended to ask the crematorium to blend the ashes with the deceased's ashes after the cremation.

Understanding Burial documentation
When a funeral director organises with a family for burial, they will need to complete an application form with the chosen cemetery. These forms may vary depending on the

cemetery's processes. If it is for a new grave, the process is straightforward. However, if you are wanting to place your loved one into a family burial plot, then permission from the burial rights holder has to be sought.

In most cases it is the deceased themselves, however, sometimes it can be a family member who is not present at the time the arrangements are made. The cemetery will guide you on who needs to be contacted. On the day of the service the funeral director hands over the application for the grave along with the copy of the Form 9 (Medical Cause of Death Certificate) or Coroner's Release for the cemetery records.

The family will then contact the chosen cemetery to arrange for a headstone to go upon the grave.

Application for a Death Certificate.
You will need to complete the *Application for a Death Certificate* form required by Births, Deaths, and Marriages.

The information required to register the person's death:

- Full name and address of the deceased.
- Where they were born.
- Date of birth, date of death, and their current age.
- What was their occupation?
- Were they born overseas and, if so, what year did they arrive in Australia?
- In Australia—are they of Aboriginal or Torres Strait Islander descent?
- Were they married, *de facto*, divorced, separated, never married or widowed?

TWELVE | Burial or Cremation

- Where they were married, how old they were, and to whom they were married. *(It is important to note that if they have been married more than once, all marriages are to be recorded. If the information is not known to you, it is best to state 'unknown'.)*
- The full names and occupations of their parents, especially the mother's maiden name.
- If they have children, their names, and dates of birth, including children who are deceased. *(You can only record the names of their birth children or their legally adopted children. If there are children from a partner's marriage, and they were not adopted by the deceased, they cannot be listed as their children.)*
- The funeral director will complete where the service was held, on what day, and who the priest or celebrant was.
- The funeral director will contact the deceased's doctor or hospital, or the Coroner's Office, to obtain the 'Form 9 Medical Cause of Death Certificate' or 'Coroner's Release'. *(This is **not** the official death certificate.)* This certificate or coroner's release is required by law, and the original will be sent to Births, Deaths, and Marriages along with the Death Certificate Application form. Births, Deaths, and Marriages will then produce the official death certificate to be sent to the family.

When a person is to be buried, unlike cremation, it will not matter what items are placed in the coffin. However, the cemetery is never happy if they find out that another person's ashes are interred in the coffin. It is best to notify the cemetery to find out about their policies beforehand. You will also need to inform the funeral director if the family wish to be pallbearers. If not, the funeral company has to ensure they have enough staff to pallbear for you.

When a person is to be placed in a monumental gravesite it will be arranged for a monumental mason to remove the monument from the grave. The cemetery will advise you on what has to be done.

Families who have a crypt or tomb have some additional processes to undergo:

- The deceased will need to be embalmed
- The deceased will be placed into a lead-lined coffin
- There will need to be a copper tray to go under the coffin in the crypt/tomb.

Once again, the cemeteries involved will pass their requirements onto the funeral director, and the family, at the time of arranging the burial.

The funeral director will want to know if you would like to have a religious service with the family priest or pastor from your local church, or a non-denominational service, i.e., with a funeral celebrant. Most funeral companies have a list of funeral celebrants that they can match with the family.

There is also nothing stopping you from organising your own celebrant. You should advise the funeral director if you

TWELVE | Burial or Cremation

have a preferred celebrant who you would like to perform the service. Or, you may have a family member who feels comfortable enough to do the service themselves. There are no hard-and-fast rules, you just need to be comfortable with who you want to lead the service.

CHAPTER THIRTEEN

Choosing the Celebrant, Priest, or Pastor

One of the most important parts of any funeral service is the choice that is made with regards to a celebrant or religious clergy. With a religious service held in a church there will be a set way the priest, minister, or pastor will do things. They will adhere to their doctrine, with some family input. Where there are occasions that the service is held in the funeral home or crematorium chapel with a religious minister or priest, the service will be similar to a church service with some minor adjustments.

A funeral celebrant is a non-denominational leader for a service. They sit with the family and support the family with options on how they would like the service to come together. The celebrant will be there on the day and will run the service. The celebrant can help the family with ideas to prepare eulogies and, if no one is able to speak at the funeral, they will deliver the written word on behalf of the family. Most funeral companies have a list of funeral celebrants they can recommend; they also have direct contact with local churches and ministers to organise dates and times for services. Also, bear in mind there is no reason you cannot source the celebrant yourself, or you may ask a family member or friend who has the confidence, to present the service.

The funeral celebrants I have suggested to families were almost always well received. However, I had one occasion where I had to 'dismiss' one, but he and I talked it through at the time and reached an understanding. I was still finding my way as a funeral arranger, and the celebrant I chose was one of the best around—and he still is. When he met with the family, he could tell he wasn't gelling with them. The next morning the family rang and asked me to find someone else. They said there was nothing wrong with him and he was a good celebrant, but he wasn't 'their kind of people'. Luckily for me, the celebrant took the rejection well and was understanding about it.

We had a retired Uniting Church minister who worked with us, and I rang him to see if he was available. When I rang the family to say he would be in touch I did warn them he may turn up in his gardening clothes. The family laughed so much at this and, sure enough, he did arrive in his gardening clothes. The family fell in love with him, and the service was beautifully presented. It taught me to be more in-tune with who, and what, the family wanted.

Over the years, I developed a technique of showing families the business cards of the celebrants I used. I would ask them to look at the photo and see who they felt most comfortable with, and to use their intuition. I would advise new celebrants how important it was to have their photo on their business card. Not just for the family to see their faces, but also the family would be able to recognise them when they showed up at their front door.

CHAPTER FOURTEEN

Prearranging Your Funeral.

My personal experience with organising my mother's funeral was, to say the least, mind-boggling! Our mother's answer to all questions relating to death was just, '*Chuck me under a stump in the back yard when I am gone*'. Filling in the paperwork for Births, Deaths, and Marriages brought up some angst between me and my sister.

Luckily for me, I was researching the family tree at the time. My grandmother's maiden name was the first hurdle. All of our lives we knew our great aunts' maiden names was McGrath, however, our grandmother and her twin were born *out of wedlock* and were registered under my Great Grandmother's maiden name of Mantell. Again, it was lucky that the funeral director was a cousin to my mother, and he could confirm this with my sister, who had some difficulty processing all the different names.

When speaking with families about prearranging, I advise them that the most important things a funeral director will want to know are:

- Do you want to be cremated or buried?
- They will ask the questions relating to Births, Deaths, and Marriages, so having your family history recorded somewhere for your family is helpful.

- Also, if there have been multiple marriages and you don't know all the details, it is best you relate to the funeral director that the deceased has been married before but the information to be written is *unknown*.
- Giving false information on the application for Births, Deaths, and Marriages is a fineable offence.

This was one of the mistakes our family made regarding my mother's information at the time of her death. Because she had been in a *de facto* relationship with my stepfather for over 25 years, she had used his surname. All her medical and Medicare records carried that surname. However, she had never changed her name legally to Burgess, and she really should have been registered by her current legal surname of Porter. Throughout my career I learnt that we can't use our emotions when registering a death.

Prepaying your funeral - there are a few options available

- **Prepaid funerals:** All funeral companies have some sort of prearranged/prepaid funeral plans. Some are *guaranteed price* plans, and some are *contribution towards* plans. They are both good options, and they allow you to record your wishes with the funeral company, to hold on file. The downside is if you move from your current residence, you may not be able to transfer your plan to another funeral company without some sort of penalty. These are things you need to discuss with the funeral company when you take out the policy.

FOURTEEN | Prearranging Your Funeral

- **Funeral Bonds:** Personally, I have a funeral bond with *Sureplan Friendly Society*. This is, by no means, a recommendation, it's just an example to share with you. The bond allows my family the flexibility to choose the preferred funeral company when the time comes to arrange the funeral; and it is not locked into a particular area of Australia. I have invested a lump sum for both my husband and me, and each year the bond pays interest that is compounding and will help towards the rising cost of funerals. There are many insurance companies and banks that offer Funeral Bonds.

    Sidenote: at the time of printing, aged pensioners in Australia are allowed to have up to $14,000 in a funeral bond for each person before it is considered an asset. This amount changes yearly and is set by the Department of Social Services. It is always best to speak with your financial advisor first before setting up a bond as you move towards retirement.

- **Funeral insurance:** Now we have all seen those advertisements on television talking about the rising cost of funerals, and how this insurance will pay for a funeral for as little as a cup of coffee a day. Funeral insurances allow you the flexibility to choose your own funeral company, and there are no restrictions on where the funeral is held.

    My experience with funeral insurance companies is that they pay out within 48 hours of making a claim—providing they receive the correct documentation. Funeral insurance, unlike a funeral bond, is a life insurance policy, so the terms and conditions need to be looked at closely.

For instance, a gentleman approached me for an update on the cost of a funeral. He had a life-threating illness and wanted to put things in place for his children's sake. From our conversation, he realised his funeral insurance policy would not cover the funeral service that he wanted.

He then approached the funeral insurance company to increase his policy. What he was not clear on at the time was that his policy increase was then considered to be a new policy and would only pay out the amount on *accidental death* within the first *two years*. Sadly, he passed away within six months, and his children were devastated to learn that the company would not pay out that amount for which they thought their father was insured.

I understand that, after much discussion with the Office of Fair Trading, they were given the sum that he was originally insured for. Unfortunately, it did not go anywhere near covering the cost of the funeral.

I always made it quite clear to families who had funeral insurance, not to change or cancel the policy. Alternatively, they could set up something the children could access, such as a funeral bond, or

FOURTEEN | Prearranging Your Funeral

put funds into a separate, designated bank account. The downside to holding money in a separate bank account for aged pensioners in Australia, is that Centrelink deems bank accounts as an asset. Again, forward planning and advice from your financial planner on these matters is recommended.

CHAPTER FIFTEEN

Don't let your story die with you

I could not finish my book without reiterating the need to let your family know how you want to be farewelled.

Start by recording your family history and your most memorable moments.

On my own journey, I started researching my family tree: growing up in a blended family I always wanted to know about my roots and where I came from.

I was *that* girl at school who had a different surname to the one on her birth certificate. At school, my mother had registered me under her current husband's surname of Porter. However, my birth certificate showed my surname as Kelly, which was my mother's husband's surname from her first marriage.

One day a lovely man came to visit us, and mum introduced him as her 'brother'. Now I know I was only 11 years old, but things just didn't make sense to me, because I knew my mother was an only-child. I was later to learn that he was my biological father. As I had been born out-of-wedlock somewhere between the two marriages, my father was classed as *Unknown* on my birth certificate.

To say my family history was complicated would be an understatement! In the past few years, with the introduction of DNA testing via *ancestry.com*, I was able to confirm that my 'Uncle Charley' was indeed my birth father. The DNA match was conclusive.

So, let's get started

My suggestion is to get started by recording *your* personal history and *your* preferences for a fond farewell.

- Firstly, record your parents' names, your place of birth your marriage/marriages, and your children's names and birthdates (as discussed in Chapter Twelve).
- Make sure the family know if your preference is for burial or cremation.
- Write down, or make a recording of, some of your special moments in life.
- What are your favourite things?
- Talk to your family and tell them the stories about the mischief you got up to.
- Put your photo albums together.
- Ask your children to write down some things they may like to say about you.

Whatever you do, please don't leave this world without leaving behind your story.

I will share with you some of my favourite things, I love: sunflowers—they remind of my great-grandmother; spending time with my family; and hugging my grandchildren.

FIFTEEN | Don't let your story die with you

When my time on this earth has ended, I will not let my story die with me.

Will you?

Resource Library

I have listed some useful resources below, which will help you to plan a fond farewell—whether it is for a loved one, or perhaps even for yourself.

Pre-Paid Funerals

Sureplan Funeral Friendly Society
www.sureplanfuneralinsurance.com.au/products/funeral-bond

Guardian Plan
www.guardianplan.com.au/

Funeral Plan Management
www.fpmanagement.com.au/

Finding a funeral director

Try an internet search on funeral directors in your local area or visit these Australia-wide sites.

Australian Funeral Directors Association
afda.org.au/

Independent Funeral Directors of Australia
www.funeraldirectorsaustralia.com.au/

National Funeral Directors Association of Australia:
nfda.com.au/

Cemeteries and Crematoriums

Australasian Cemeteries & Crematoria Association (ACCA)
accaweb.com.au/

Finding a Celebrant

Australian Federation of Civil Celebrants
www.afcc.com.au/

Help for Grief Counselling

Try an internet search for local grief support groups or counsellors in your local area or visit the following sites for advice.

Beyond Blue
www.beyondblue.org.au/

Lifeline
www.lifeline.org.au/community-counselling/

About the Author

Rita-Marie Lenton

Rita-Marie Lenton grew up in rural Queensland, Australia, and her own life story is one of triumphing over adversity, and the gift of forgiveness. However, *Creating a Fond Farewell* examines understanding the choices and options we have ... when someone dies.

A long and fascinating career as a funeral director and crematorium manager has prepared Rita-Marie to write *'a long overdue and informative book to help people negotiate the worst time of their life'*.

She is a contributing author to several books, and this book, *Creating a Fond Farewell*, is her first foray into writing a book as the sole author.

Rita-Marie lives on the beautiful Redcliffe Peninsula in Queensland with her husband David and high-maintenance and media-savvy pet cat, *Sweetie*.

Acknowledgements

Never in a million years did I think I was good enough to write a book, let alone have the courage to start.

'The journey of a thousand miles starts with the one step.'
                                                                Lao Tzu.

I want to thank my husband, David, who supported me while I worked long hours in my chosen career, and when I decided finally to lock myself away in my office to write this book. I thank my children, and grandchildren, who inspire me every day.

I want to thank Carissa and Steven Pretsel for allowing me to share Baby Kiara 'Wolfey' Pretsel's story, also Don and Julie Sager for allowing me to share Adam Sager's story. I felt honoured by the trust they placed in me, and the friendship they extended to me beyond the funerals.

I wish to acknowledge the incredible people I have worked with over the years, especially Bill Wiggins for the mentorship and support he gave me. *Rest in Peace* now, my friend.

I also want to thank Nerida Thompson, Annette Lourigan and Carla Hitchcock for the continued love, support, encouragement, and friendship you have given me throughout the years. I am also grateful to all the funeral staff I have worked with over the years—far too many to mention—especially those that supported me during my time as a manager.

While I have not named the two companies that employed me throughout my career, I am eternally grateful for the employment they gave me, the experiences I had, and the opportunity to look after the families in our care.

I want to thank the beautiful people in my life who have encouraged and challenged me, at every turn, to write my stories. The three main ladies of our 'MBCC committee days': Deborah Fay of Disruptive Publishing, Trish Springsteen, author, mentor and coach, and my editor Joanne Scott. I value these ladies as loyal friends, who saw the author in me long before I recognised her myself.

I also want to thank my friend Frances Cahill for helping me through the initial drafts to make sense of some of my ramblings.

Last, but not least, I acknowledge and honour all the families who I have helped throughout my career. It has been a privilege and an honour.

Thank you from the bottom of my heart.

More by the same Author

Rita-Marie is a contributing author to several compilation books in the genres of self-development, emotional wellbeing, and spirituality.

See more from Rita-Marie in these publications:

Touched by Breast Cancer, compiled by Trish Springsteen

Forever Changed by Suicide, compiled by Trish Springsteen

Keep up to date with Rita-Marie via social media:

Australian Federation of Civil Celebrants
www.afcc.com.au/celebrant/rita-marie-lenton/

Facebook
www.facebook.com/Soulcrystalearth

Instagram
www.instagram.com/soulcrystalearth/

LinkedIn
https://www.linkedin.com/in/rita-marie-lenton-4109b196/

Website
www.soulcrystalearth.com.au/

What's Next from Rita-Marie?

Following her retirement as a funeral director, Rita-Marie has embarked on an exciting new career as an authorised Civil Celebrant. Her business, *SoulCrystalEarth,* is based in the beautiful Moreton Bay region of Queensland.

Her passion is to bring family and friends together to celebrate and honour special moments in life. She draws from her professional knowledge and vast life experiences to create the perfect ceremony, whatever the occasion.

Whether it be a wedding, a renewal of vows, or saying a fond farewell to a loved one, Rita-Marie gently works with her clients to achieve the best ceremony for their needs.

www.ingramcontent.com/pod-product-compliance
Lightning Source LLC
Chambersburg PA
CBHW042349300426
44109CB00035B/137